1|5|14

Louisburg Library District No. 1

206 S. Broadway

Louisburg, KS. 66053

913-837-2217

www.louisburglibrary.org

STRANDED!
Testing the Limits of Survival

Lost in a
DESERT

by Meish Goldish

Consultant: Marie Long
Arizona-Sonora Desert Museum
Tucson, Arizona

BEARPORT
PUBLISHING

New York, New York

Credits

Cover, © Maridav/Shutterstock, © Tom Wang/Shutterstock, © Julien Hautcoeur/Shutterstock, © SCOTTCHAN/Shutterstock, and © Aleksey Stemmer/Shutterstock; 4, © Stronger/AFP/Getty Images; 5, © Mauro Prosperi; 6, © Pierre Verdy/AFP/Getty Images; 7, © John Kund/The Image Bank/Getty Images; 8, © Merek Velecjovsky/Shutterstock; 9, © Radius/Superstock; 10, © Incredible Arctic/Shutterstock; 10B, © Tobkatrina/Shutterstock; 12L, © Snehit/Shutterstock; 12R, © MBOE/Shutterstock; 13, © Patrick Poendl/Shutterstock; 13R, © Image Broker/FLPA; 14C, © Deon Reynolds/Iconica/Getty Images; 14B, © Pershing County Sheriff's Office; 15, © Ethan Miller/Getty Images; 16, © AP Images; 17, © U.S. Air Force/U.S. Department of Defense; 18CR, © Dr. James Hubbard; 18B, © GFC Collection/Alamy; 19, © Kravka/Shutterstock; 20BR, © AP Images; 20–21, © Adstock/Shutterstock; 21, © Carr Clifton/Minden Pictures/FLPA; 22C, © Craig Brewer/Photographers Choice/Getty Images; 22BR, © Animals Animals/Superstock; 23, © AP Images; 24CL, © Victoria Grover; 24–25, © Claudio Del Luongo/Shutterstock; 25C, © Samphire Photography; 26, © Alan Majchrowicz/Photolibrary/Getty Images; 27, © Stace Hall; 28, © Nic Neish/Shutterstock; 29, © Frans Lanting/FLPA.

Publisher: Kenn Goin
Senior Editor: Joyce Tavolacci
Creative Director: Spencer Brinker
Photo Research: Brown Bear Books Ltd

Library of Congress Cataloging-in-Publication Data

Goldish, Meish.
  Lost in a desert / by Meish Goldish.
      pages cm.—(Stranded! Testing the Limits of Survival)
  Includes bibliographical references and index.
  ISBN 978-1-62724-285-1 (library binding)—ISBN 1-62724-285-6 (library binding)
  1. Desert survival—Juvenile literature. I. Title.
  GV200.5.G65 2015
  613.6'9—dc23
                             2014004644

For more information, write to Bearport Publishing Company, Inc., 45 West 21st Street, Suite 3B, New York, New York 10010. Printed in the United States of America.

10 9 8 7 6 5 4 3 2 1

Contents

Storm in the Sahara

In the spring of 1994, Mauro Prosperi took part in a **grueling** six-day race called the Marathon of the Sands in the North African country of Morocco. The 39-year-old Italian police officer, along with 133 other runners, set out to race 151 miles (243 km) across the hot and sandy Sahara Desert.

Every year, runners from around the world take part in the Marathon of the Sands.

4

Mauro knew the race would be very tough. Temperatures in the desert can easily soar to 120°F (49°C). What Mauro didn't expect, however, was a **sandstorm**!

On the fourth day of the race, millions of grains of sand whirled in the air. They pounded and stung Mauro's skin. To keep the sand out of his mouth, eyes, and ears, Mauro wrapped a scarf around his face and head. "I needed to keep moving," he said. If he didn't, Mauro felt like the blowing sand would bury him alive.

Mauro Prosperi

The Sahara Desert

Morocco

Sahara Desert

AFRICA

Atlantic Ocean

Indian Ocean

The Sahara Desert is the largest desert in the world. It stretches across many countries in Northern Africa, and is about as big as the United States.

Lost!

For six hours, the powerful sandstorm made it almost impossible to see. When the winds finally died down, Mauro was lost. He saw no other runners and there was no trail—just endless mounds of sand. Mauro had no idea which way to go. Although he was afraid, he didn't panic.

A powerful sandstorm blowing across the Sahara Desert

Race organizers told Mauro and the other runners not to move and to wait for help if a sandstorm struck. However, Mauro continued to walk during the sandstorm and accidentally wandered far off course.

Mauro stayed in the same spot and waited for someone to find him. He fired a **flare gun** high into the desert sky, hoping someone would see his signal. Yet no one came. The next day he saw a helicopter—but it flew past him. After running out of food and water, Mauro became very weak. Large birds called vultures circled above him. He decided he had to take matters into his own hands in order to make it out of the desert alive.

In the desert, vultures swoop down to eat dead, injured, or sick animals.

Desperate to Drink

Tired and aching, Mauro forced himself to walk across the dry, hot desert. "All I could think about was that I was going to die a horrible death," he said. By the third day, he was **desperate** for water. He caught two bats, twisted off the animals' heads, and drank their blood. For the next five days, he **trudged** on. Each morning, he licked **dew** off the leaves of desert plants.

Mauro also caught and ate snakes and lizards, such as this gecko.

Because the temperature in a desert can reach 120°F (49°C), people must drink a lot of liquid to stay cool. Without it, they will grow weak and die of **dehydration**.

Dying of thirst, Mauro drank tiny drops of water that he found on desert plants.

Finally, after being **stranded** a total of nine days and walking more than 130 miles (209 km), Mauro was spotted by a group of desert **nomads**. He was very weak and had lost nearly 42 pounds (19 kg). Mauro was taken to a hospital, where he later recovered. Despite the frightening experience, Mauro continues to run races in the Sahara. "I love the desert—it's stronger than me," he said.

Mauro was found by Tuareg (TWAH-rehg) nomads, a group of people who have lived in the Sahara Desert for thousands of years.

What Is a Desert?

The Sahara Desert, where Mauro Prosperi nearly lost his life, is just one of many deserts around the world. However, not all deserts are filled with sand like the Sahara. Many deserts are rocky. Others are covered with steep jagged cliffs. Not all deserts are hot, either. Some deserts are cold—or even freezing.

These ice-covered mountains are located in a desert in a part of the world called the Arctic.

Death Valley, in the Mojave Desert in California, is one of the hottest deserts in the world.

The two largest, coldest deserts in the world are the Arctic and the Antarctic. These areas are called **polar** deserts. Each is a **barren**, frozen land covered with ice. Although a cold desert is very different from a hot desert, all deserts have one thing in common: they are areas where little or no rain falls.

Deserts Around the World

Arctic Ocean

NORTH AMERICA

Escalante Desert

Great Basin Desert

Mojave Desert

Sonoran Desert

Chihuahuan Desert

Atlantic Ocean

EUROPE

Sahara

AFRICA

ASIA

Karakum

Gobi Desert

Taklimakan

Thar

Arabian Desert

Pacific Ocean

Pacific Ocean

SOUTH AMERICA

Sechura Desert

Atacama Desert

Namib Desert

Indian Ocean

AUSTRALIA

Australian Desert

Patagonian Desert

Kalahari Desert

Southern Ocean

ANTARCTICA

N W E S

- ⬛ Desert
- 🟰 Arctic Polar Desert
- ▦ Antarctic Polar Desert

Deserts cover about one-third of Earth's land surface.

Desert Plants and Animals

Because deserts have such little water, few people live in them. However, some types of plants **thrive** in deserts. For example, **cacti** need little water to **survive**. When it rains, the plants store the water they need in their thick, waxy stems. Some cacti can live off this water for many months.

A large saguaro cactus can hold up to 2,000 pounds (907 kg) of water.

A barrel cactus

Animals in the desert have found ways to survive with very little water. For example, in the Sahara, camels can live for more than a week without drinking water. A kangaroo rat never has to search for water. It gets all the water it needs from eating moist seeds. Many lizards and other **reptiles** are also well suited to desert living. Some, like the chuckwalla, store water in their tails.

A kangaroo rat

Like many desert animals, the kangaroo rat stays underground during the day to escape the desert heat. At night, it comes out to search for food in the cool air.

A chuckwalla

The hump on a camel stores fat that the animal's body uses to survive when there is little or no food.

Struggling to Survive

Although many plants and animals can survive in a desert, the same is not true for people. In March 2012, James Klemovich and Laszlo Szabo drove into a **remote** Nevada desert to go exploring. Suddenly, their car became stuck on an **isolated** road. They tried to get it moving again, but the car wouldn't budge. Making matters worse, there was no cell phone service in the area. The men lit flares and small fires, hoping to draw someone's attention.

The area of the Nevada desert where James and Laszlo became lost

James Klemovich (left) and Laszlo Szabo (right)

As the hours passed, James and Laszlo grew thirsty. They found some rainwater in a ditch, but it was too dirty to drink. Luckily, James remembered some survival skills he had learned as a Boy Scout. He cleaned the water by **straining** it through a towel. Now the men could drink—but would they ever be rescued?

In some deserts, like the one in Nevada where James and Laszlo were stranded, snow sometimes falls in winter months or in early spring.

The desert in Pershing County, Nevada, where James and Laszlo were stranded, covers 6,000 square miles (15,540 sq km). However, fewer than 7,000 people live there.

Keeping Alert

Four days passed. Still, no one came to rescue James and Laszlo. Anxious and afraid, Laszlo left the car to look for help. James stayed behind, hopeful that someone would find them. Hunger **pangs** shot through his belly. He tried to stay calm and alert by keeping a journal. Each day, however, he became more worried.

Joanne Klemovich, James's wife, holds a photo of herself with James. She never lost hope that he would be found.

The days passed slowly. One week later, Laszlo was still gone. James was barely hanging on. Finally, soldiers who were training in the area discovered the car. Help had arrived! The soldiers gave James food and took him to a hospital. Sadly, Laszlo did not survive. His body was found in the desert a mile and a half (2.4 km) from the men's car.

U.S. soldiers training in Nevada

Despite being hungry and thirsty, James did not have any major injuries. He soon recovered in the hospital and then returned home to his wife.

Lessons Learned

A desert can be a deadly place for anyone lost there. Why did James survive while Laszlo did not? Dr. James Hubbard, an expert on survival skills, says that James was smart to stay in the car. He saved energy by remaining in one place.

Dr. James Hubbard

In the desert, a car can serve as a shelter. It can help protect a person from the extreme weather outside.

Laszlo, however, walked around the desert, using up valuable energy. Without enough water to drink, Laszlo became dehydrated. Dr. Hubbard thinks that this may have caused him to grow confused and become lost while trying to find his way back to the car.

According to Dr. Hubbard, Laszlo should have placed markers, such as small rocks, every few feet as he walked. This would have helped guide him back to the car.

Water can mean the difference between life and death in a dry desert.

A Rough Journey

James Klemovich survived ten days in the desert on mostly water. Yet people who are stranded for much longer also need food to survive. William LaFever learned that lesson in June 2012 while hiking in the Escalante Desert in southern Utah.

The Escalante Desert

William LaFever

William planned to walk from Boulder, Utah, to Page, Arizona—a distance of more than 90 miles (145 km). Although he knew the journey would be tough, he didn't realize he'd be risking his life.

The sun blazed as William crossed the rocky, hilly land. He hiked along the Escalante River, stopping often to drink. Eventually, his body grew tired and weak. He needed food but had brought very little with him. How would he make it all the way to Arizona?

The Escalante River

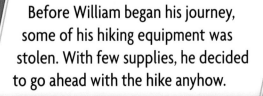

Before William began his journey, some of his hiking equipment was stolen. With few supplies, he decided to go ahead with the hike anyhow.

Finding Food

In desperate need of something to eat, William dug up and ate the roots of desert plants. He also caught frogs in the river and ate them raw. With so little to eat, however, William hardly had the energy to keep on walking. After three weeks, he had lost 50 pounds (23 kg) and was near death.

Some desert plants found in the Escalante Desert have roots that can be eaten.

William ate frogs, such as this northern leopard frog, to survive.

By the time a rescue helicopter spotted him, William had collapsed in the river. He was too weak to walk and could barely raise his arm to wave to the helicopter for help. The helicopter's crew was sure he wouldn't have survived another day. They had found him just in time.

Amazingly, William had managed to hike 40 miles (64 km) through the desert before he collapsed.

William was flown by helicopter to a hospital, where he recovered after treatment.

A Bad Break

As William LaFever discovered, surviving in a desert is not easy. Yet what about surviving in a desert with a serious injury? Victoria Grover faced that emergency in April 2012. While hiking alone in southern Utah, she jumped off a short **ledge** and landed on a rock. She felt a rush of intense pain as her ankle buckled underneath her. Victoria knew right away that she had broken her leg.

Victoria Grover

The desert area in Utah where Victoria went hiking

Unable to walk, the 59-year-old woman worked quickly to make a **splint** with her walking stick. Then Victoria dragged herself on her hands and knees to a nearby creek for water. To avoid the desert heat, she slept in the shade all day long. At night she faced another challenge—extreme cold. How would she survive?

Victoria had broken her leg above the ankle. She made a leg splint with her walking stick, similar to this one.

Because Victoria worked as a doctor's assistant, she knew how to make a splint for her broken leg. The splint held her leg in place to prevent further injury and help lessen the pain.

Staying Tough

"The worst thing is the cold," Victoria said. At night, the temperature dropped to near freezing. Even with a **poncho**, which she used as a blanket, Victoria shivered nonstop. After a few days, she was suffering from **hypothermia**, a dangerous condition that left her sleepy and confused. For four days, Victoria remained stranded by the desert creek.

The area of Utah where Victoria was stranded

Victoria developed hypothermia because her body temperature dropped dangerously low in the cold desert air. A body temperature below 95°F (35°C) can lead to death if not treated immediately.

Finally, police located Victoria. "What a relief . . . to find her alive," said one of her rescuers. "I certainly could have died out there," said a thankful Victoria.

Deserts can be deadly places. People such as Mauro Prosperi and Victoria Grover, however, have learned what it takes to survive in such extreme conditions. They now know to always be prepared and to never give up—no matter what.

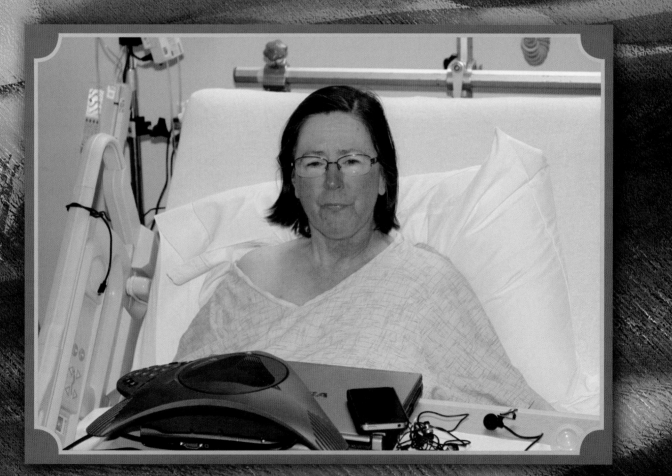

Victoria was rushed to a hospital, where she regained her health. From her hospital bed, she said that she would continue hiking.

Desert Survival Tips

If you plan to visit a desert, follow these tips to help you survive.

- ☑ Tell people in advance where you are traveling and when you plan to return.
- ☑ Bring a cell phone with plenty of extra batteries.
- ☑ Carry extra food and water, in case you get stranded.
- ☑ Bring enough clothing and a sleeping bag to stay warm during cold desert nights.
- ☑ Bring matches to start fires in order to stay warm or to alert people that you need help.
- ☑ In the desert heat, drink water regularly so you do not become dehydrated.

A survival kit should include things such as a cell phone, a flashlight, and a first-aid kit.

- ☑ Find shade to protect yourself from the sun. If you must be out in the sun, wear sunscreen, a large hat, light-colored clothing that covers your body, and sunglasses.
- ☑ Try to move in the early morning or just before it gets dark. During these times, you will stay cooler and save energy.
- ☑ Keep away from dangerous desert creatures such as spiders, scorpions, and snakes. Keep your skin covered by tucking in your pant legs to lessen the chance of getting stung or bitten.
- ☑ If a sandstorm occurs, close your eyes or put on glasses. Cover your nose and mouth with a cloth or handkerchief to protect your lungs from the sand. Keep your back to the wind so the sand does not blow directly in your face.

A desert scorpion has a curved poisonous stinger at the end of its tail.

Glossary

barren (BA-ruhn) having few trees or plants

cacti (KAK-tye) plants that have thick fleshy stems or pads covered with sharp spines that grow in hot, dry areas

dehydration (dee-hye-DRAY-shuhn) dryness in the body caused by a lack of water

desperate (DESS-pur-it) feeling hopeless; willing to do anything to fix a situation

dew (DOO) small drops of water that collect overnight on cool surfaces

flare gun (FLAIR GUN) a gun used to produce a blaze of fire or light

grueling (GROO-uh-ling) very demanding and tiring

hypothermia (hye-puh-THUR-mee-uh) a condition where a person's body temperature becomes very low

isolated (EYE-suh-*lay*-tid) far from settlements with people

ledge (LEJ) a narrow, flat shelf on the side of a mountain or cliff

nomads (NOH-mads) people who move from place to place

pangs (PANGZ) sudden brief pains

polar (POH-lar) relating to the icy areas near the North Pole or South Pole

poncho (PON-choh) a coat that looks like a blanket

remote (ri-MOHT) far away; distant

reptiles (REP-tilez) cold-blooded animals that have dry, scaly skin, a backbone, and lungs for breathing

sandstorm (SAND-*storm*) a strong windstorm that carries clouds of sand

splint (SPLINT) a piece of wood, plastic, or metal used to support an injured limb

straining (STRAYN-ing) pouring through a screen or other filter to separate solids from liquids

stranded (STRAN-did) left in a strange place

survive (sur-VIVE) to stay alive during or after a dangerous event

thrive (THRIVE) to grow or to do well

trudged (TRUHJD) walked slowly with effort

Bibliography

Johnson, Mark. *The Ultimate Desert Handbook: A Manual for Desert Hikers, Campers, and Travelers.* Camden, ME: Ragged Mountain Press (2003).

Men's Journal Editors. *Wild Stories: The Best of Men's Journal.* New York: Broadway Books (2003).

Nester, Tony. *Desert Survival: Tips, Tricks, & Skills.* Flagstaff, AZ: Diamond Creek Press (2003).

Read More

Jackson, Kay. *Explore the Desert (Fact Finders).* North Mankato, MN: Capstone (2007).

Rice, William B. *Survival! Desert (A Time for Kids).* Huntington Beach, CA: Teacher Created Materials (2012).

Sandler, Michael. *Deserts: Surviving in the Sahara (X-treme Places).* New York: Bearport (2006).

Learn More Online

To learn more about surviving in a desert, visit
www.bearportpublishing.com/Stranded!

Index

About the Author

Meish Goldish has written more than 200 books for children. His book Disabled Dogs *was a Junior Library Guild Selection in 2013. He lives in Brooklyn, New York, where the Brooklyn Botanical Garden has a large display of desert plants from around the world.*